A group of large pots made by Vicki Read of Claycutters Studio, Winslow, Bucks, the tallest 28 inches high, dolomite and magnesia glazes over and under oxides and slips, reduction fired in a gas kiln to 1,300 degrees Centigrade.
COVER: *A candle holder made by the author. 16 inches high, in two pieces, it has a cream felspar glaze with iron banding.*

CRAFT POTTERY

Thomas Plowman

Shire Publications Ltd

CONTENTS

Begin at the beginning	3
What is craft pottery	5
Clay—the potter's body	7
The clay takes shape	11
Decoration	17
Glazing	21
Firing the kiln	25
Back to the beginning	31

Printed in Great Britain by City Print (Milton Keynes) Ltd, Denbigh Hall, Bletchley, Bucks.

For Polly, Julius and Benedict—J.G.D.

Copyright © 1976 by Thomas Plowman. First published 1976; reprinted 1980. Shire Album 18. ISBN 0 85263 347 5.

All rights reserved. No part of this publication may be reproduced or transmitted in any form or by any means, electronic or mechanical, including photocopy, recording, or any information storage and retrieval system, without permission in writing from the publishers, Shire Publications Ltd, Cromwell House, Church Street, Princes Risborough, Aylesbury, Bucks, HP17 9AJ, UK.

ACKNOWLEDGEMENTS

Photographs are acknowledged as follows: Crafts Advisory Committee, pages 3, 5, 8 (left), 9 (right), 10 (top), 20, 24 (top left and bottom), 25, 32 (top); Craftsmen Potters Association of Great Britain, pages 7 (both), 9 (left), 30 (bottom); Thomas Plowman, pages 2, 11, 13 (both), 15 (all), 16, 17, 19 (all), 23, 26 27, 29 and cover; Andrew Priddy, pages 8 (right), 31; Vicki Read, pages 1, 21, 24 (top right); Eileen Stevens, page 32 (bottom); Stephen Wolfenden, pages 10 (bottom left and right), 30 (top).

Most potters identify their work by impressing a stamp on or near the base of their pots. The author's two stamps, shown here, denote his name and the location of the workshops at Stalham in Norfolk.

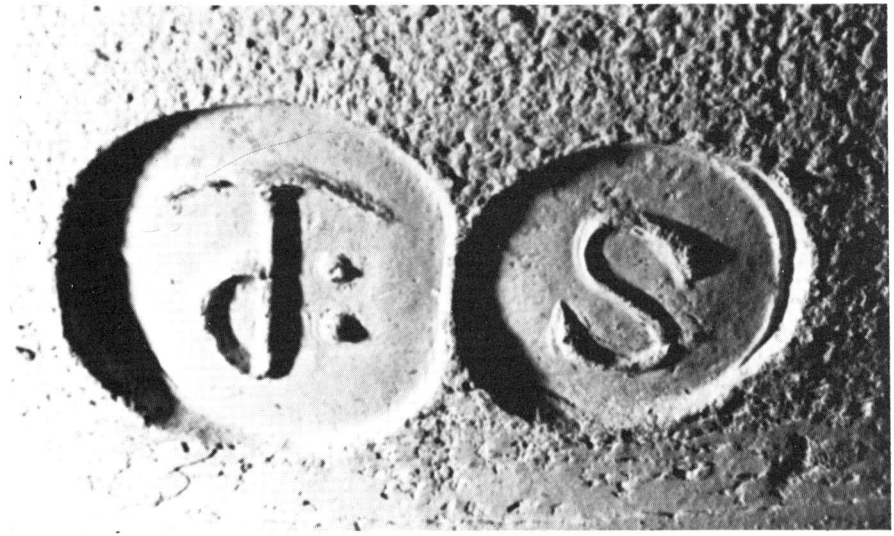

A jar and a mug by David Leach.

BEGIN AT THE BEGINNING

Knowledge, like the potter, is a two-handed beast; the left hand of knowledge is experience and the right hand is theoretical understanding and they are, naturally, complementary. One without the other leads to a lop-sided, incomplete view of things. Experience, you will note, comes first on the left hand because that should always if possible be the order of things. It gives a taste of the real thing through feeling and intuition before the conscious mind becomes too set. The purpose of this little homily is to impress upon the reader the value of carrying out the suggestions contained in this first chapter.

Before I go any further with this book I want you, the reader, to gain some experience of pottery—not by getting your hands on the raw clay (although that is a very sound way of experiencing), but by getting familiar with the pottery in your immediate surroundings.

Collect together on the table a representative piece of all the kinds of pottery you have in the house. It will almost certainly include something other than the earthenware of modern factory production—maybe some porcelain or a stoneware vase. What do these terms mean? Do not think about them for the present, but give your attention to the pottery in front of you. Are the pieces light or heavy relative to their size? What colours are the glazes, and are they shiny or matt, rough or smooth? What colour is the clay that gives form to the pot? Look underneath the pot as there is nearly always a small unglazed area, even if it is only the foot ring. Is the texture of the clay close or coarse? If the clay is exposed and buff to reddish brown, try putting a drop of moisture on it. If the moisture obviously soaks in to the fabric of the pot, indicating porosity, that tells you something quite particular about the pot.

There are many qualities to observe even in the most modest collection. Browse amongst the array in front of you. Do not try to think too hard about them, but just let some impressions float into your mind. It is amazing how much we can assimilate if we do not try to focus our attention too closely.

Now that you have looked at some of the qualities of the material from which the pots have been made, turn your thoughts to how they have been formed. Again, are they heavy or light relative to their size? Do they have fine or heavy furrows in spiral rings on the sides or are they completely smooth? Are the pots round or oval or irregular in shape? Is there any sign of a seam or join that might suggest that the pieces were cast in a mould? Look closely, all around and underneath, to see if there is any name or sign stamped or incised on them. Are they, in your opinion from this growing experience, crudely fashioned or finely made? If you have two of a kind, how exactly similar are they? Most important, which of all the pottery in front of you do you like the best? Have you any ideas why you should choose one against another?

All these questions and injunctions are not included for you to answer or carry out specifically. They are just a few stimuli to help you to turn your attention towards some of the possibilities contained in the field of pottery. As you have no doubt already realised, the cup of knowledge overflows.

A bowl in reduced stoneware and boxes in reduced porcelain, all wood-fired, by Gwyn Hanssen.

WHAT IS CRAFT POTTERY?

As you can imagine from your brief look at the pottery in your immediate surroundings, the range of types of pottery is enormous. There are many areas of specialisation in the subject, from the history through aesthetics to the purely technical, quite apart from the activity of producing the goods. This small book could not possibly cover the whole range and so it must serve as a light introduction to one aspect of ceramics – craft pottery. It might be subtitled 'How to ask intelligent questions when you visit a pottery'. The intention is to give the basis of an intelligent approach to the subject, for the pleasure we gain from any experience increases with the growth of understanding.

Craft pottery, in the sense that I wish to write of it, is a twentieth-century phenomenon, with beginnings in France and England as early as the middle of the nineteenth century. The mainstream of its growth can be traced directly back to Bernard Leach at St Ives, Cornwall, where he set up his pottery in 1920. There were other notable influences at work as well, not the least being William Staite Murray, who began work in London early in this century, but it was from the Leach pottery that so many active practitioners came. Of course, so many aspects of present-day craft pottery bear no relation to that 'tradition' in the type of work produced or in its philosophical standpoint. However, the seminal influence of St Ives and its early incumbents is undeniable and of enormous importance.

Craft pottery is best defined by the work produced in the many small pottery workshops which have come into being throughout the British Isles. These workshops are often established and run by a craftsman working entirely alone, carrying out all the processes from clay-mixing to selling his pots directly to the public. He is turn by turn labourer, artist, technician, artisan, salesman, administrator and much more besides. It would be well remembered when visiting him that the demands of his job are rigorous and the time he gives you is given generously, so try not to abuse his generosity, however interesting it may be to stay and chat. He will value above all your genuine appreciation of his work. The workshops seldom employ as many as ten craftsmen and usually considerably fewer. Where they do exceed that number, a division of labour generally takes place, the pottery produced takes on a more stereotyped look, and there is a loss of personal identification between pot and potter. This type of pottery workshop, for the purposes of commercial expediency, may superficially imitate the style of craft pottery, as indeed much factory-produced pottery has also begun to do in recent years, but these products fall outside my definition of craft pottery.

Craft pottery is that work which is produced in small workshops, with each piece being identified with one craftsman or a small group of craftsmen working in an integrated way with each other, and so giving the resultant work its own characteristic quality.

That so many craft pottery workshops have sprung up is a phenomenon not confined to the British Isles but is part of a world-wide new growth of interest in the crafts. When you next see a pot being made by hand in one of these small workshops, you might speculate upon the wider social implications of what you witness. The activity of making pots by hand in the second half of the twentieth century is not an anachronism. It is an activity which expresses a desire for identity in the things we own and a reassessment of the values that have produced our current way of life.

In these small workshops is produced an array of pottery of enormous range in style, material and imagination. Most of it is suitable for use, even if the use is non-specific, and it is with this type that I wish most to concern myself. Ceramic modelling and sculpture employ materials and fabrication methods in common with craft pottery, but their *raison d'etre* begins from a different point.

Quality in work is almost impossible to define. It is possible, however, to have some guidelines about the standard of craftsmanship, in the narrower sense of the term. If, for instance, a jug is ill balanced for pouring or a lid does not fit reasonably well, then it would be fair to say that the piece of work was not well made. But then a piece may measure up to all the practical criteria and yet be a very dull thing indeed. Alternatively, the bizarre shapes made perhaps in an attempt to be completely original do not display a mature imagination at work. Within the confines of this book there is not enough room for a discussion on the discernment of creative imagination at work, but in the following chapters describing the transformation of a piece of lumpen clay into a finished glazed pot there will, it is hoped, be hints towards the development of true appreciation.

LEFT: *Stoneware with a talc glaze and sgraffito decoration, 14 inches high, by Raymond Finch.*
RIGHT: *Stoneware with matt white, breaking orange glaze, and incised decoration, 27 inches high, by Alan Wallwork.*

CLAY—THE POTTER'S BODY

It is common knowledge that pottery is made from clay. It is its very specific qualities of structure and behaviour that make clay so suitable as a material for pottery-making. It is slippery when wet, yet sticky at the same time, as you will know if you have ever tried putting a spade into it. It has the property of taking up water when it is dry but becoming somewhat water-resistant when it is wet. One of its most valuable attributes is its plasticity, that is the capacity for being moulded or formed. When potters speak of plastic clay they are not referring to some artificial substance dreamed up by the petrochemical industry but to clay which is malleable and most useful to the potter. The property of plasticity in clay comes mainly from its plate-like particle structure. In a small piece of clay there are millions of tiny flat plate-shaped grains, all surrounded by a film of moisture, each sticking to their neighbours and capable of sliding about over each other, maintaining adhesive contact. This gives the clay the behavioural characteristic that enables it to take up a shape on the potter's wheel in a most dynamic way. The other main quality of clay is the chemical change it undergoes when subject to intense heat. Water is

LEFT: *A tin-glazed earthenware goblet by Alan Caiger Smith.* RIGHT: *A three-pint, cane-handle stoneware teapot with iron and cobalt brush decoration, in pale green high-silica glaze, reduction fired to 1,320 degrees Centigrade, by David Winkley.*

driven off and the particles, mainly of silica and alumina, form tight bonds that render the material strong and durable. The two most dramatic changes that clay undergoes in the process of becoming a piece of pottery are, first, the change from formless lump to hollow vessel, perhaps of great beauty, and then transformation from dry clay pot, friable and weak, to hard fired durable pottery.

There are many kinds of clay, not all of which are suitable for making pottery. Some are too heavily contaminated with other material, rendering them useless; others melt at too low a temperature, and so on. The selection by the potter of the right clay for the job is most important. He usually refers to his clay as the 'body', meaning the material, which may be a blend of a number of different clays and other substances which most suits his needs. Potter's clay falls into three general categories, as does pottery itself, but there are many exceptions to these brief notes which are intended only as a rule-of-thumb guide when looking at clays and types of pottery.

Earthenware. The clay in its raw state can be any colour from light buff to dark reddish brown and is usually highly plastic. It is fired to temperatures of up to 1100 degrees Centigrade. A guide to visualising such heat is that the hottest embers of a bonfire are 750-800 degrees, so temperatures above that are very hot indeed. Because of the way it is fired, earthenware clay remains porous to a greater or lesser degree, and so it is usual for most of the surface of the pottery to be covered with an impervious layer of glaze. The lower temperature of the glaze firing makes it possible to use a wider range of colouring materials, and so earthenware is usually characterised by a bright, shiny surface. The more traditional type of earthenware is slipware,

LEFT: *A stoneware piece with impressed decoration and felspathic glaze, 3¾ inches high, by Richard Batterham.* RIGHT: *A group of porcelain vases from 9 to 11 inches high, in grey pink glaze with white stripes, by Val Barry.*

made from terracotta clay and decorated with liquid clays or slips underneath the glazed surface.

Stoneware. This is the most popular range of pottery for the craft potter. Clays range in the buff to brown category in their unfired state, becoming light buff to grey on firing, depending upon the treatment in the firing and the amount of iron oxide in the clay. Normally fired between 1,250 and 1,300 degrees Centigrade, stoneware forms a hard, dense non-porous basis for all kinds of ceramic products from drainpipes to eggcups. Because of the great temperature at which it is fired many of the materials that produce colour in glazes cannot be used as they would volatilise, so the tonal range of the finished pottery is generally limited to the more subtle shades of colours similar to those found in pebbles on the beach. This quiet tonal range is also contributed to by the fact that at these high temperatures there is much more interaction between body and glaze; this has the effect of modifying the base colour of the glaze and also accounts for the characteristic flecking of brown spots, similar to a thrush's egg, on the surface of the glaze.

Porcelain. This is the finest kind of pottery, fired usually at temperatures in excess of 1,280 degrees Centigrade and made from bodies containing a high proportion of china clay; the result is a hard, non-porous, close-textured, white type of pottery. One of the most attractive qualities of porcelain is its translucency; if the cross-section of the pot is thin enough it will transmit some light and this imparts an overall effect of delicacy and fineness. Porcelain has become in recent years an area of great interest and experimentation for the craft potter.

LEFT: *A jug in reduced stoneware by Michael Casson.* BELOW LEFT: *A breadcrock in reduced stoneware with dolomite glaze, fired to 1,300 degrees Centigrade, and 12 inches high, by Biddy Rose.* BELOW RIGHT: *A candle house in reduced stoneware, with green glaze, fired to 1,300 degrees Centigrade, 8 inches high, by Diana Rose.*

Throwing—forming a pot on the wheel. Note the use of water to lubricate the hands and the few simple tools—sponge, chamois leather, calipers and trimming tool.

THE CLAY TAKES SHAPE

Throwing. This is the name given to the method of forming pots on the potter's wheel and is undoubtedly the best-known, for there are few people who have not seen it demonstrated, either directly or on television. It is the most widely used way of making pots in craft pottery for many reasons. Perhaps the foremost is that it is a fairly quick process and so enables the potter to produce work at a fast enough rate for him to offer domestic pots at reasonable prices and still make a living. So often when the throwing technique is demonstrated, people ask how long it takes to make a pot. The answer, for a small item like a mug, is approximately two minutes, that is to throw it, but you will appreciate that it goes through many other processes before it is finished. 'Throwing' seems an odd word to use and has been the source of too many jokes; it really describes the initial move in forming a pot on the wheel. The clay, suitably prepared, free from trapped air bubbles and of the right consistency, is patted into a ball and thrown in the centre of the turning wheel. Using water to lubricate the contact between clay and hands, the potter applies pressure to ensure that the lump spins centrally. Then by pressing his thumbs into the clay he 'opens up' the pot. Further squeezing causes the clay to thin out and the pot begins to take shape. The final form depends upon a number of factors including the potential of the clay, the skill of the thrower and the quality of imagination the potter brings to his craft. The best thrown pots are not necessarily those which display the highest mechanical skill in their making. In the minutes that pass whilst a clay lump becomes a pot the potter, in a most dynamic way, creates a concrete expression of his creative imagination. Whatever decoration, glaze or other treatment the pot may receive subsequently, it carries with it the quality of the initial impulse. Perhaps this is the other main reason why throwing is such an important method of forming pots, for no other way offers quite the same degree of immediacy.

Coil building. This is a relatively slow method of forming pots, in direct contrast to throwing. Clay is made into long rope-like lengths and the shape is built up coil upon coil, each ring pressed into contact with the one immediately below. It is a very simple method, basically requiring only clay and skilled hands, yet it offers a most subtle approach to pottery-making. In the slow build-up of the shape the original idea has time to mature and grow along with the pot. Many potters have developed this method with great skill and produced tools and techniques to a high degree of refinement. Coiling can be used as a way of making pots of cyclopean proportions, not possible by other methods, or it can be used for making very fine coiled and pinched pieces where the fabric of the pot becomes almost eggshell thin.

Pinching. This is a way in which pots, usually fairly small, are formed out of a solid lump of clay. A ball of clay is held in one hand and then a depression is made with the other hand. Gradually the fingers pinch the clay out thinner and thinner and the pot grows. The control of the shape is done by gently teasing the clay in the direction desired. It requires great delicacy of touch and is often used for making small pieces of porcelain. The resultant forms are usually asymmetric and often inspired by or derived from shapes which occur in plants, fungi and other natural phenomena.

Slabbing. This term, like so many in pottery, is self-explanatory. Pots are made from slabs of clay. The clay is rolled out into slabs of equal thickness, rather in the way that piecrust pastry is prepared. The pieces needed for any particular shape are then cut out and joined together to create the desired form. The clay, being malleable, will take up a curve quite readily and so the variety of shapes possible is endless. With this particular method potters frequently prepare a special 'body' which reduces the shrinkage of the clay and enables the pot to retain a precise shape as it dries and is fired. The potter is frequently asked what glue he uses to join the pieces together. The joining is done without the use of any adhesive, as clay is its own adhesive – clay sticks to clay. To ensure the bond between two pieces, some slip is placed at the join and pressure is applied, in much the same way as glue would be used in joining two pieces of wood. Slip is clay which has enough water added to it to form a thick liquid, the consistency of cream. It has many uses in pottery-making, but is particularly useful when one piece has to be attached to another, as with spouts, handles, knobs, lugs and joined sections.

Moulding. All pots which are formed by clay taking up the shape of a matrix fall into this category, but the actual methods vary enormously. At its very simplest level is the one-piece press mould. A shape, usually of an open dish, is cast in plaster of Paris,

LEFT: *Removing the excess clay from the base of the pot is called turning or fettling. This is done at the leather-hard stage.*

BELOW: *A box of potter's tools! Small sponges, thin-bladed knives, fine wire-cutters, hole-makers, boxwood spatulas, and useful things from the kitchen.*

and then clay, rolled or cut into flat slabs, is placed over the mould and then pressed to the contours of the mould; then the excess clay is cut away. The resultant shape is allowed to dry and in so doing shrinks free of the matrix. This method has been extended to include more complex shapes, and sometimes pieces are press-moulded in two or more pieces and subsequently joined in much the same way as described for slabbing. The limitations are that the shape must not place too great a demand on the forming characteristics of the clay and must allow free withdrawal from the mould. More complicated shapes are moulded by using the slip-cast method. Slip, being clay in its liquid form, can take up any shape. Provided that the clay from which the slip is made is fine enough it can reproduce fine surface detail as well as overall shape. Many potters have again and again seen their own fingerprints inadvertently reproduced on slip-cast pots. The moulds for slip-casting are also made of plaster of Paris, which absorbs the moisture in the slip, and in this way a coating of clay is built up on the inside of the mould. The complexity of the shape of the pot determines the number of pieces of the mould, from two upwards. With slip-casting offering such fidelity to the potter's original design, you might think it would appeal the most. But, perhaps just because it imparts a rather mechanical quality to the pots, most craft potters, with some notable exceptions, use it little or not at all.

These are the principal ways in which the craft potter imparts the original shape to his wares. Of course, in working practice the methods do not fall neatly into categories. A pot may be subject to a whole mixture of methods to arrive at its finished form. For instance, a box may be built by the slab method and have a series of thrown pieces attached to it, knobs, handles, foot ring and so on. Alternatively, a basic thrown shape may have all manner of additional work done on it by one method or another and the final form may bear small resemblance to the original shape. It is up to the potter to use whatever techniques he has at his disposal with skill and imagination. His failure or success is embodied in a durable object and so he should be mindful of what he brings into the world. To produce an everyday object like a teapot requires a range of skills: first the throwing of the parts, body, lid and spout; then perhaps turning the body and fitting the lid; cutting the spout and fitting it, not forgetting the strainer holes; making and attaching the handles; decorating, glazing and firing. Moreover all the parts must be done in relation to each other so that the finished pot is a homogenous whole, much more than a collection of its parts. The considerations are both functional and aesthetic, so a teapot may stand as an object of beauty in its own right.

OPPOSITE PAGE. TOP LEFT: *Attaching the handle to a jug. The clay stub is pressed on to the pot using a little slip at the join to ensure a good bond.*

TOP RIGHT: *Pulling the handle. Using water to lubricate the hand, the clay is gently stroked out to the correct length and then joined at the base.*

BOTTOM LEFT: *Spouts are placed in position after being cut to shape and are joined to the body of the pot whilst the clay is still soft enough to work with a wooden tool.*

BOTTOM RIGHT: *A group of large jugs with recently made handles. Handles and knobs are attached when the pots are at the leather-hard stage, that is firm to the touch yet still moist.*

Pots packed ready for a bisque firing in an electric kiln. Note that pots are stacked inside and on top of each other.

A group of porcelain teapots by the author. Pots must be allowed to dry out completely before bisque firing.

DECORATION

It is quite impossible, in general terms, to give a step by step description of how a piece of clay becomes a pot, because the potter has many options open to him at every stage. A precise description of the evolution of a lump of clay into an object of beauty would only be possible if we took a particular pot and traced the history of its formation back to its beginnings. The matter of decoration is a case in point. Decorative techniques are available at every stage of the pot's formation up to the final glaze firing and it would be pedantic to argue about the point at which decoration begins. To those who have a classical sense of beauty the pure form and unblemished glaze of a finely made piece of porcelain, for instance, are decorative enough themselves and any further application of pattern would only detract from its purity. However, there are quite specific techniques of decoration and a few words about some of them will give an idea of the range available.

Painting. To be strictly accurate, the potter's palette consists not of paints but of pigments. It is a fine distinction but is made to draw the mind away from the normal idea of paint as a covering layer. With the exception of enamels, the potter uses colouring materials which have an interaction with the glazed surface of the pots during their final firing. The pigments cannot be made from any organic material because they would be burnt away during the intense heat of the firing, so more stable, permanent colouring agents are used. They are most commonly metallic oxides, iron, copper, cobalt and manganese being the most widely used in craft pottery. These oxides are mixed with water and some neutral material such as white ball clay as a base and painted on to the pot either under or over the glaze. When fired, the pigment modifies the glaze colour in the area it has been painted and so we see it as a painted decoration.

Slip decoration. The slips (liquid clays) are also coloured with either naturally occurring or added metallic oxides. The slip is either painted on or more commonly piped on with a tool called a slip trailer. The technique bears some relationship to icing a cake and one of the best slip decorators I have seen at work was a confectioner turned potter. This method is especially suitable for linear designs and motifs which stand out from the surface of the pot.

Wax resist. This is the technique of painting with hot wax on the surface of the pot. The area thus painted **resists** any further application of pigment, slip or glaze, and so retains the colour of the material over which it was painted. Wax resist painting is used to very good effect when a pot is given two coats of glaze. The pot is first coated with, let us say, an ochre glaze, then the hot wax pattern is painted on, and finally the pot is coated with a contrasting green glaze. In the places where the wax has been painted the green glaze will not take, and so when the pot is fired the wax melts away and the decoration is revealed in the original ochre glaze, whilst the rest of the pot displays the colour resulting from the combination of green glaze over ochre glaze.

Sgraffito. This word, borrowed from the Italian, means to scratch or score. A pot is coated with slip or pigment and then a design is put on to the pot by scratching or scoring away the upper surface to reveal the original colour below. This is sometimes done as a direct linear drawing to produce a concrete image and sometimes by cutting away contrasting areas to form abstract patterns.

Sprigging. This is the method of placing an embossed design on a pot. The appearance is of the design slightly raised from the surface of the pot with the detail in low relief. The intended design is cut into a block of plaster of Paris or a cast is taken from an original in clay. When the matrix is ready, clay is pressed into it and the excess cut away. The three-dimensional relief design is then lifted from the mould with a palette knife and applied with slip to the surface of the pot. A variation on this is to apply clay directly to the pot and cut or model a design into the raised surface directly. Figures and objects are sometimes

OPPOSITE PAGE: *Four pots by the author.*

TOP LEFT: *A small lidded box, with creamy white glaze, brush decorated with pigment bearing iron and copper oxide.*

TOP RIGHT: *A box with cut lid; made as a cylinder with a flat top, the lid is cut with a fine-bladed knife when leather-hard.*

BOTTOM LEFT: *A flared-top bottle with a wood-ash based glaze. The vertical fluting is cut into the pot with a boxwood tool whilst leather-hard.*

BOTTOM RIGHT: *A lipped wine jar, 8½ inches high, decorated with double glazing and wax resist technique. The four facets were beaten on the body of the pot whilst it was still damp.*

freely modelled on to the pot in a further extension of this technique.

There are so many ways of adding to the interest of the shape and surface of a pot that this has in itself been the subject of books much longer than this. In the interest of decoration and in order that the potter may indulge his fascination with the endless variety of forms the final pot may take, so much happens to the humble clay. A bowl may be no more functional than when it is perfectly round, but it may be beaten or squashed square whilst the clay is still wet, or it may be fluted or faceted, painted or pinched, or, if the shape is pure and strong, left to stand untrammelled, all in the cause of giving the creative imagination full play. I have among my collection of ceramic objects a chimneypot taken from a demolished Georgian house. Made by hand, it has two bands of decoration of crowns and stars around its rim. Why should it be decorated in this way when it was to spend its life high up on a London roof seen only by the pigeons? I suppose the decoration was put on it because its maker felt intuitively that it was right to do so – it somehow completed the job. Perhaps that is the best criterion we can bring to our appreciation of the potter's art – that the pots at their best stand as they are because to be less than they are would be incomplete and to be more would be superfluous.

A large stoneware plate with iron brush decoration, by William Marshall.

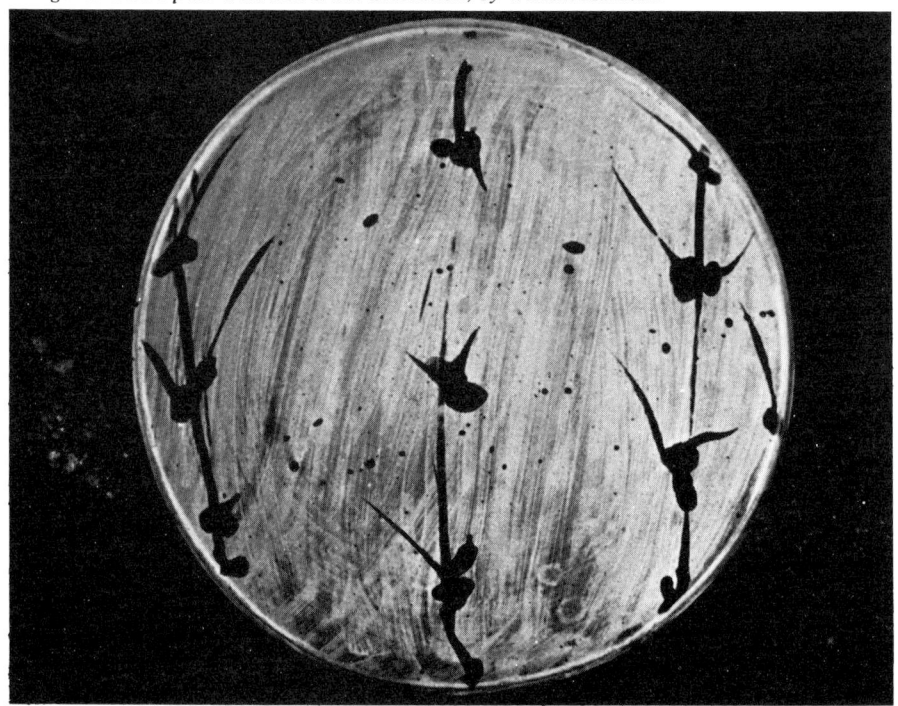

A platter bowl, 12½ inches across, with a magnesia glaze over a stock glaze, and copper oxide giving a faint blush, by Vicki Read.

GLAZING

Without glaze pottery would be a much lesser thing. Put in an oversimplified way, glaze is glass and glass is made from fused silica. Now let us examine that more closely. Glaze performs a number of functions, but foremost it offers a hard, impervious coating to the body of the pot, rendering it non-porous in the case of earthenware, and makes it durable and easy to clean. It is also the means by which colour, texture and finish are imparted to the pot, which takes us back to the difficulty of distinguishing between what is function and what is decoration. The most suitable material to form the basis of glaze is silica, but silica melts at the relatively high temperature of 1,710 degrees Centigrade and if a glaze was made of pure silica then the pot and the kiln would become molten before the glaze had fused! So other earth materials are added as fluxes, that is they lower the melting temperature of the silica. The maturing temperature of the pottery to be fired determines the composition of the glaze and the type of fluxes used.

Other materials are present in glazes for quite specific reasons, as in the case of alumina. When a glaze is fired in the kiln it reaches maturity by becoming molten and so all its particles fuse into a glass-like surface. At the time of fusion the glaze becomes a liquid. Liquids have the tendency to find their own level and, unless something is added to glaze to prevent it, the glaze would all slide off the pot when it was fired and form a pool on the shelf of the kiln. Alumina has the property of thickening the liquid and thus arresting the tendency of the glaze to flow and so it prevents such problems from arising.

It is difficult to describe further the composition of glazes without becoming too technical, but many other substances are added to the composition of glazes for the purposes of colour, texture, hardness, thermal shock resistance and so on. Often these substances are present in commonly found materials and it is quite normal for a glaze formula to be simple from the point of view of a non-technical potter as opposed to a ceramic chemist. Very beautiful glazes can be made from equal parts of clay and wood ash and this juxtaposition of common materials was probably the way in which glaze was first discovered. Nevertheless an analysis of the various constituents of wood ash and clay would reveal the presence of silica, alumina, soda, potash, iron oxide and much more besides.

How is the glaze applied to the pot? The various constituents are placed together in a tub and mixed with water. They are then passed through a sieve to remove and break down any large lumps (large in this case being anything much bigger than a grain of salt). The tiny particles do not mix with the water but are merely suspended in it. A pot is then taken in its porous state and dipped in the glaze. The porosity of the pot absorbs some of the water and an even coat of glaze is deposited on the outside of the pot. The water evaporates and leaves the pot with a powdery coating all over its surface. The glaze at this stage is all there in its essential ingredients but has not yet been fused by the heat of the kiln. It now requires the intense heat to cause all these tiny particles of silica, alumina and so on to melt together and form the clothes of the pot, covering and enhancing all the work that has gone into the pot so far.

Glaze may also be applied by spraying and painting, but this is a rare practice in craft pottery workshops.

The other notable type of glazing is salt glazing. The essential elements of the glaze are retained, but the method of application differs in quite a dramatic way, so justifying a separate description. With salt glaze part of the constituents of the glaze arrive on the pot by being borne on the gases that pass through the kiln. Unglazed pots are placed in the kiln and fired in the normal way until a temperature of approximately 1,250 degrees Centigrade is reached. Then salt is thrown on to the fire and the heat causes it to volatilise and pass through the kiln as a vapour. The sodium of the salt makes a bond with the silica present in the clay of the pot and forms a sodium silicate glaze coating on the pot. The glaze only forms where the passing gases of the kiln have been in contact with the pot.

OPPOSITE PAGE: *Getting the glaze on to the pot by dipping. The porous pot sucks in the water and the glaze forms a coating on its surface.*

TOP LEFT: *A slab bottle in reduced stoneware with Tenmoku glaze, 7½ inches high, by Bernard Leach.*
TOP RIGHT: *A 'swan pot', with block decoration in oxides under a dolomite with wood-ash glaze, 10½ inches high, by Vicki Read.*
LEFT: *A hand-built stoneware pot with painted slip decoration by Elizabeth Fritsch.*

A globular speckled glazed pot, 10 inches high, by Barbara Cass.

FIRING THE KILN

No amount of skill and no degree of facility in the potter's art are of much use without the application of heat to make them permanent. The firing of the glaze kiln is truly the final, irreversible transformation. But even here we have the possibility of variation in the application of general principals. Up to the point where the pot has been made and all the clay work finished everything holds good. The pot is allowed to dry until practically all the moisture has gone from it. During this drying time the pot shrinks as the moisture leaves it. It has reached the point where it must be fired to make it durable and for this a kiln is needed, with a means of heating it. The kiln, very simply, is an insulated box into which pots can be placed and heat generated. Pots have been fired by the use of every kind of fuel, but craft potters usually use gas, oil, electricity or, if a suitable supply is available, wood.

Now it must be decided whether to fire the pots once or twice. If the pot follows the most common practice it will be twice fired and the first firing is called the biscuit or bisque firing. The purpose of this process is to cause the clay to undergo a chemical change, to drive off the chemically combined water and realign the molecular bond so that the previously fragile dry clay pot becomes strong

and durable, yet remaining open-textured and porous. This last-mentioned quality is to facilitate the application of the glaze. The pots are packed into the bisque kiln one upon another, small ones inside larger ones and so on. Care has to be taken in the way the pots are arranged, but the bisque kiln, with skill, can be densely packed. The heat is built up very slowly at the beginning and is advanced steadily to somewhere between 900 and 1,000 degrees Centigrade. Too rapid a rise or too sudden a change in rate of rise of temperature during the firing can cause the pots to crack, so great care is taken. It depends greatly upon the type of pots, kind of clay and size of kiln how long the firing takes, but a total firing cycle is rarely less than twelve hours to build up to full heat and perhaps twice that time to cool down.

When the bisque firing is completed, the pots are glazed and may be decorated also at this stage. They are then repacked into the glaze or glost kiln. The glaze will become molten at the height of the glost firing, therefore no two pots must touch, neither must any glazed area of a pot come into contact with the kiln shelves or it will become irretrievably stuck. Then the unpacking can only be done with a hammer and chisel and the result would be a box of fragments and ruined kiln shelves! So care is taken in packing each pot close to its neighbour, but not touching. The firing then proceeds, usually faster than the bisque schedule, but just as steady until the top temperature is reached. At this point the glazes flux and fuse. The kiln may be held at this top temperature for a while to allow the glaze to mature before the heat is shut off and cooling begins. Again the kiln and its contents are cooled slowly and the potter must wait to see how well he has done his work and how kind nature has been to him.

The atmosphere of the kiln plays a part in determining the colour of the fired clay and glaze. You will hear potters speak of pots fired in either oxidising or reducing atmospheres. These terms refer to the amount of oxygen available in the kiln while combustion of fuel takes place during the firing. If a kiln has an oxidising atmosphere that means that the fuel can take all the oxygen it needs for full combustion to take place. If, on the other hand, pots are fired in a reducing atmosphere, then there is not enough free oxygen in the kiln for full combustion to take place. The flame becomes 'hungry' for oxygen and so draws upon some of the oxygen contained in the oxides that form part of the fabric of the pots and the glazes and pigments. This causes them to undergo chemical changes which we see at the surface level as changes in colour. For instance, iron oxide in a glaze fired in an oxidising atmosphere produces a range of colours from tan to brown. The same glaze fired in a reducing atmosphere at stoneware temperatures (1,250–1,300 degrees Centigrade) would produce green.

Raw glazing is another term you may come across. It refers to the practice of firing the glaze on to pots which have not had the benefit of bisque firing, so both firings are done at once. This has the economic advantage of using less fuel per pot, but the range of glazing possibilities is much diminished.

Enamels are applied to the glazed surface of the pot and then fired on at temperatures in the region of 700 degrees Centigrade. In this way very bright colouring materials and gold and silver can be added to the surface of the finished pot. These low-temperature enamel colours would otherwise be burnt off in the extreme heat of the glost firing.

PRECEDING PAGES, LEFT: *The inside of the glaze kiln before it has been fired. The powdery unfused glaze hides the decoration and surface interest of the pots.* RIGHT: *The same glaze kiln after firing when the glazes have all fluxed and the decoration on the pots has been revealed.*

Checking the kiln during the glaze firing. A reducing atmosphere in the kiln is indicated by the flames coming from the upper spyholes.

LEFT: *A reduced stoneware vase with dolomite glaze, 12 inches high, by Diana Rose.* BELOW: *Stoneware in matt white, rubbed copper and matt black, 9½ inches high, by Robin Welch.*

A cut-sided teapot of 1½ pints capacity, in reduced stoneware with Tenmoku glaze by David Winkley.

BACK TO THE BEGINNING

I have touched upon much in the text of this small book and left a great deal more unsaid. I hope it has been of interest to those who previously knew little or nothing of the craft of the potter and maybe has stimulated the wish to read further. But first of all go back to the beginning of this book and look at your pots again to see if your appreciation has in any way gained in breadth or depth. If it has stimulated you to ask many questions about craft pottery which this book does not answer, then that is good.

There are as many variations of practice of the craft as there are potters working. No two work exactly alike because each is an individual in his own right and therefore displays his own special brand of creativity through his work.

In our culture we have, perhaps, overemphasised the verbal aspect of thinking and have wrapped up so much of our experience in neat conceptual packets. As a guide to the appreciation of craft pottery let me suggest that in quietness you allow the pots to tell you something about themselves in their own non-verbal tactile way. Handle the pots and examine them closely and, above all else, enjoy them. Practical things which owe more than

A hemisphere of reduced stoneware, 8 inches across, by Joanna Constantinidis.

mere utility to their existence have a way of impinging upon your consciousness through regular daily use. In a collection of pots it is interesting to see which ones go on giving pleasure and gaining in discernible quality and which ones fail to live up to their initial promise. Naturally enough, those pots which are immediately eye-catching and exciting are not always the ones that live on. Mere excitement is a short-lived emotion and, if that is all that the pot embodies, then it is no surprise that it should pall after a while; but then quiet little pots may be quiet just because they are dull. There are no rules for appreciation except that you must be awake to the immense range of possibilities by being awake in yourself. I hope this has been a small bridge to a journey of great discovery and enjoyment.

A stoneware wine set with apple-tree wood-ash glaze, by Eileen Stevens.